D1467296

{ Little-Known FACTS ABOUT Well-Known PLACES }

TEXAS

{ *Little-Known*
FACTS
**ABOUT**
*Well-Known*
PLACES }

TEXAS

VICTOR DORFF

FALL RIVER PRESS

New York

# FALL RIVER PRESS

New York

An Imprint of Sterling Publishing
387 Park Avenue South
New York, NY 10016

ISBN 978-1-4351-3127-9

Distributed in Canada by Sterling Publishing
*c/o* Canadian Manda Group, 165 Dufferin Street
Toronto, Ontario, Canada M6K 3H6
Distributed in the United Kingdom by GMC Distribution Services
Castle Place, 166 High Street, Lewes, East Sussex, England BN7 1XU
Distributed in Australia by Capricorn Link (Australia) Pty. Ltd.
P.O. Box 704, Windsor, NSW 2756, Australia

For information about custom editions, special sales, and premium and
corporate purchases, please contact Sterling Special Sales at 800-805-5489
or specialsales@sterlingpublishing.com.

Manufactured in China

2 4 6 8 10 9 7 5 3 1

www.sterlingpublishing.com

# INTRODUCTION

This is a little book about a big place with an even bigger heart.

Just how big is Texas? Here are some statistics to put the Lone Star State in perspective:

Texas is a little bit bigger than France and a little bit smaller than Turkey.

With a land area of 263,644 square miles, Texas is the largest of the 48 contiguous states. All of New England, New York, Pennsylvania, Ohio, and Illinois could fit inside Texas, leaving more than enough room for Delaware.

The largest ranch in Texas (the King Ranch in Kingsville) by itself is slightly larger than the state of Rhode Island.

The airport at Dallas/Ft. Worth is bigger than the island of Manhattan in New York City.

But it isn't the size of Texas that makes it so great. Godzilla was big, too, but that didn't make him popular!

What makes Texas amazing is its diversity, its completeness, its independence.

Its history is all about strength and courage, full of people with ideas of their own and the wherewithal to make things happen.

And pride. Lots of well-earned pride in who they are, where they came from, and how they succeeded against daunting odds.

Enjoy!

Look for these other
titles in the series:

*Little-Known*
FACTS
ABOUT
*Well-Known*
PLACES

DISNEYLAND ✦ IRELAND
ITALY ✦ NEW ORLEANS
NEW YORK ✦ PARIS
WALT DISNEY WORLD

exas isn't as big as it used to be. When Texas first became a U.S. state, its borders stretched into what are now the states of Colorado, Kansas, New Mexico, Oklahoma, and Wyoming.

After the United States won its war with Mexico in 1848 over the annexation of Texas, the state needed money to pay off debts and to build its infrastructure.

In 1850, as part of a larger compromise between pro-slavery and abolitionist factions in Washington, Texas agreed to give up one-third of its area in exchange for $10 million.

The pact formed Texas' western border with New Mexico, creating the now-familiar Panhandle.

As time went on, Texas got smaller. When Mexico signed a border treaty with the United States in 1819, the agreement was based on a faulty map that showed the boundaries of Texas (Mexico's northernmost territory) incorrectly. The 100th meridian was drawn in the wrong place, and a fork in the Red River was missing.

After Texas became a state, that border issue became a domestic dispute. According to the faulty map, Greer County belonged to Texas. The accurate positions of the longitude lines and the river's edge put the land in the Oklahoma territories.

In 1896, the U.S. Supreme Court settled the case and helped shape the Texas border we know today.

Ruling that reality trumps a misleading map, the Court chiseled off Greer County, Oklahoma, chipping a little more territory away from Texas.

The 1848 Treaty of Guadalupe-Hidalgo between the United States and Mexico established the Rio Grande as the new international border.

In 1864, when a major flood receded, the river had moved to the south. Suddenly, a tract of land between El Paso and Ciudad Juarez that belonged to a Mexican farmer was *north* of the border. Legal ownership of the place called Chamizal caused friction between the two countries for nearly a century.

In 1964, the United States agreed to relocate more than five thousand Texans who lived in the disputed area, to cement the Rio Grand back into place along its original course, and to return Chamizal to Mexico.

The Chamizal National Memorial stands today as a monument to the diplomatic end of that long-standing border dispute.

ack in 1959, Texas had to change the lyrics of its state song, *Texas, Our Texas,* when the behemoth Alaska supplanted the Lone Star state as America's biggest by a two-to-one margin.

The third line used to be "Boldest and largest, withstanding every test."

When that boast turned out no longer to be true, the word "largest" was changed to "grandest."

Today, Texas has more miles of highway (305,855) and operating train tracks (10,743) than any other state.

In 2009, more trucks (2.8 million) crossed the U.S. border into Texas than into any other state. In addition, more than 35.5 million personal vehicles, 18.8 million pedestrians, and 6,406 trains entered the United States through Texas.

In the same year, for the eighth time in a row, Texas was the top exporting state in the country, with revenue of $163 billion.

The Gross Domestic Product of Texas is more than $1.2 billion, making it the eleventh highest in the world.

If Texas were still a nation, it would rank just below Brazil, Spain, and Canada, and just above Russia, India, and Australia.

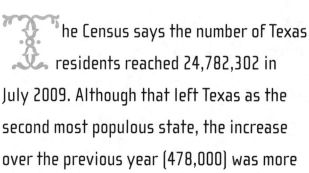

he Census says the number of Texas residents reached 24,782,302 in July 2009. Although that left Texas as the second most populous state, the increase over the previous year (478,000) was more than the growth of any other state.

Four of the nation's 10 fastest-growing cities with a population of more than 100,000 are in Texas, including Number One, Frisco.

And Texas has three of the nation's 10 largest cities: Houston (#4), San Antonio (#7), and Dallas (#9).

The Texas Medical Center in Houston is the largest medical center in the world. Founded in 1945, the Center is now the home of 25 government agencies and 24 private non-profits. Physically, with more than one thousand acres of land, the Center is about the same size as Chicago inside the "Loop." The aggregated number of gross square feet of patient care, education, and research space (about 31 million) is equivalent to the twelfth-largest business district in the United States.

A state as big as Texas couldn't possibly be satisfied with a single Official Mammal.

Instead, it has three!

- The Texas State *Small* Mammal is the armor-plated armadillo.

- The Texas State *Large* Mammal is the Longhorn (breed of cattle).

- The Texas State *Flying* Mammal is the Mexican free-tailed bat.

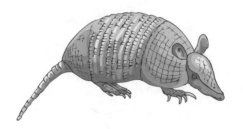

Things aren't only bigger in Texas. They're faster, too.

On rural stretches of interstate highways in West Texas, the posted daytime speed limit is 80 mph. That's the highest in the country.

At night, the speed limit drops to 65 mph.

If Texas were solely obsessed with the very large, it wouldn't have an official State Molecule.

In fact, however, there was a bit of a battle—on a very tiny scale—over which molecule to choose.

Some wanted the honor to go to the Texaphyrin. Invented at the University of Texas at Austin, it sometimes has a shape like the Lone Star on the state flag.

Instead, the Legislature chose the buckyball, or the Buckminsterfullerene molecule, which was discovered with the help of two chemists from Rice University. Made entirely of carbon, the molecule looks a lot like the geodesic domes invented by R. Buckminster Fuller, which is where it gets its name.

Both molecules have potential applications in the field of medicine and are a pretty big deal in a very small arena.

More proof that bigger is not always better in Texas:

Anyone with an interest in Chinese history, for example, can find precisely crafted, scaled-down replicas in the Forbidden Gardens of Katy, Texas.

There are nine different exhibits, including a one-third scale replica of the Terra Cotta Army of Qin Shi Huang Di. Those thousands of warriors were buried with him in the Shaanxi province to protect him in the afterlife. They were rediscovered in 1974, and scale models were made in China exclusively for Forbidden Gardens.

The Imperial City in Beijing is also on display, albeit reduced to 5 percent of its actual size. The palaces that served as home to the imperial family for 500 years are faithfully recreated to provide an insight into Chinese history without the bother of applying for a visa.

Texas is home to one of the most biologically diverse regions in the world: the Big Thicket. During the Ice Age, glaciers pushed various ecosystems from all over the continent together into a single region of what is now Southeast Texas. Today, it is not uncommon in the Big Thicket to find swamps next to sand dunes next to forests next to plains.

The economic forces that created today's Texas took their toll on the Big Thicket, which was at one time in danger of facing its own extinction. Today, however, the area is protected as a national preserve (the first of its kind) within the National Park Service and has been designated an International Biosphere Reserve by the United Nations.

TEXAS
FACTS

Eastern Texas is the home of four national forests (Angelina, Davy Crockett, Sabine, and Sam Houston) and five state forests (E.O. Siecke, I.D. Fairchild, W. Goodrich Jones, John Henry Kirby, and Paul N. Masterson Memorial).

Collectively, this massive forest area is called the Texas Piney Woods, and it is the heart of the state's lumber industry.

Naturally, the region is a perfect place for Bigfoot to spend some time (if there *is* a Bigfoot).

The Texas Bigfoot Research Conservancy is one of several organizations looking into the issue.

Not surprisingly, Texas produces more cattle than any other state, but some of the other categories Texas leads are a little less obvious.

More than three-quarters of the land in Texas is farmland, meaning it has more farmland than any other state.

Three times as much cotton comes from Texas as the next largest producing state, Georgia.

Texas is tops in the hay department, too.

And with the production of more goats and sheep than any other state, Texas is the number one wool supplier in the country.

Throughout the history of the Republic of Texas, there were no chartered banks in the country.

When the first Texas state constitution was drafted in 1845, it *prohibited* the incorporation of banks.

Banking functions were performed by financial agents and other business firms.

After the Civil War, banks began to flourish in Texas.

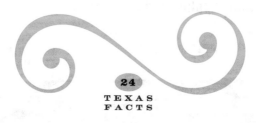

To stop a rash of bank robberies in the 1920s, the Texas Bankers Association established the Dead Bank Robber Reward Program. Anyone who killed a bank robber caught in the act would be paid $5,000. Capturing a bank robber alive would not be rewarded.

Despite a number of cases of murders staged to look like the foiling of a bank robbery, the offer of reward was not withdrawn until 1964.

To increase ridership, 19th-century railroad executives decided to stage a spectacular head-on crash of two locomotives in Texas. Everyone loves to watch a train wreck, they reasoned, and they could charge people $2 for a ticket to the crash site.

Experts determined that it would be safe to ram two steam engines together at a combined speed of 90 mph, so the railroad laid some tracks and built some grandstands just north of Waco. Then, it started advertising.

On September 15, 1896, nearly 50,000 people are said to have gathered to bear witness to just how wrong those experts were.

The locomotives' boilers exploded on impact, killing several spectators and wounding even more, effectively ending the use of an intentional train wreck as a marketing tool forever.

At least two Texas sons are said to have flown in heavier-than-air crafts well before the Wright brothers managed to get theirs off the ground.

In the late 1890s, W.D. Custead of Waco built an airship more than 30 feet long, with flapping wings. Some local residents said they actually saw it fly. Custead went on to form a partnership with another would-be aviator in New York City, but the project never went anywhere.

In 1901, Burrell B. Cannon of Pittsburg, Texas, took inspiration from the biblical story of Ezekiel and built his own flying machine. After testing it, the mechanic (and part-time minister) loaded his craft onto a flatbed railroad car bound for St. Louis (where he hoped to entice investors), but a storm destroyed the vehicle before it got there.

The first licensed black pilot in the world was also the first black woman to fly in the United States, and she was born in Atlanta, Texas.

In 1921, Bessie Coleman had to go to France to earn her pilot license, because no flight school in the United States would accept her.

She returned to the States and performed as a barnstormer, appearing in Texas for the first time in 1925.

She died during a test flight in 1926.

The U.S. Postal Service issued a commemorative stamp in Coleman's honor in 1995.

In every year from 1992 to 1997, Dallas-based Southwest Airlines, one of the nation's most consistently profitable airlines, had the best on-time performance, the least lost baggage, *and* the fewest customer complaints, as measured by the U.S. Department of Transportation. Referred to as the industry's "Triple Crown," this combination of accomplishments is something that no other airline had ever accomplished for a month, let alone for five years in a row.

The airline celebrated this event by creating a trophy and awarding it to itself each year.

When the supersonic transport known as the *Concorde* landed in the United States for the first time, it was at Dallas/Ft. Worth Airport in 1973. The occasion was the opening of the airport, and it was hosted by Dallas-based Braniff Airlines.

In 1979, Braniff became the only U.S. carrier to operate the *Concorde*. In a unique partnership with both British Airways and Air France, Braniff pilots flew the aircraft from Dallas to New York and Washington. The European crews flew the trans-Atlantic legs to London and Paris.

Although the aircraft was designed to fly at twice the speed of sound, Braniff's flights over land were restricted to subsonic speeds.

The Braniff *Concorde* flights ended in 1980, because the public showed little interest.

TEXAS
FACTS

Although some guy named Marconi gets all the credit, a Texan was really the first person to send a message by wireless radio.

Robert Stewart Hyer was a professor of physics at Southwestern University in Georgetown when he attended an 1891 Harvard lecture series on electricity and electromagnetic waves.

Intrigued, he returned home and did some work of his own.

In 1894, he sent a wireless message a distance of about a mile—from his lab to the city jail.

Hyer went on to do some early experimentation with X-rays and developed a device, which he called the "resistograph," to find oil wells.

The first film to win a Best-Picture Oscar was first shown in Texas.

*Wings*, a World War I action movie with spectacular aerial "dogfight" scenes, officially premiered in New York City in August 1927, but movie-goers in San Antonio had been treated to a sneak preview the previous May, because the film had been shot there (and in Camp Stanley).

With Clara Bow and Buddy Rogers in the starring roles and a young Gary Cooper cast as a cadet, *Wings* went on to win the *Academy Award for Best Picture, Production* in the first Oscar ceremonies ever held.

Famed millionaire Howard Hughes was, among many other firsts, the first person to pilot the largest airplane ever to fly—the Spruce Goose—in 1947.

Hughes, who was born in Houston in 1905, inherited the patent rights to an oil drill tool. He went on to make his own money as an aviator, an inventor, and a movie mogul.

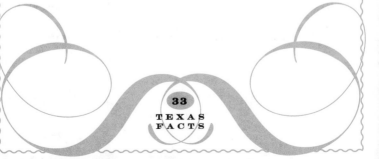

TEXAS
FACTS

Charles Elmer Doolin made candy in San Antonio during the Depression. When he first tasted a local version of fried corn chips, he was hooked. He bought the recipe and the business and made it his life's work to perfect the flavor of Fritos.

Doolin varied the recipe, created his own hybrid corn, and developed a conveyor-belt manufacturing unit to make the chips more efficiently. Along the way, he also invented the Cheeto.

In 1955, he opened the Casa de Fritos restaurants (one in Disneyland; one in Dallas).

Recipes developed for the Frito include Frito Chili Pie (invented by Doolin's mother) and chocolate-covered Fritos, but by all accounts, C.E. Doolin was a healthy eater—a vegetarian who avoided fat and salt.

The Mars candy production plant in Waco produces nearly all of the Snickers bars sold in America.

The landfills of Waco produce nearly all the fuel used to heat the Mars plant. A program designed to harvest the methane gas produced naturally by garbage puts it to good use.

As a result, Mars saves more than half a million dollars a year, and the people of Waco get to breathe a bit easier.

Texas produces more crude oil than any other state in the nation.

"Benchmarks" are used to identify various types and grades of crude oil. West Texas Intermediate, the state's signature crude, is lighter and has less sulfur than other benchmarks, and it is the major benchmark of crude oil in the United States.

The 27 petroleum refineries in Texas can process more than 4.7 million barrels each day, more than a quarter of the nation's capacity.

**P**rior to 1901, Spindletop was known as a giant underground salt dome near Beaumont. A few people thought there might be oil below it, but the experts that lived in the then-capital of the oil industry, Pennsylvania, thought they were crazy. But they kept drilling.

Finally, on January 10, 1901, the unthinkable happened. An explosive force hurled the drill pipe out of the hole on Spindletop. Then, mud, gas, and oil came flying in rapid succession. The geyser soared 150 feet into the air, and more oil than had ever been seen before in the world was literally raining from the sky.

Almost immediately, the energy economy switched from coal to petroleum, and a string of highly successful oil companies was formed to siphon the black gold from Spindletop and start searching Texas for more oil.

The eruption of Spindletop in 1901 came as such a surprise to the drillers that they were unprepared to catch the oil.

About 850,000 barrels of oil were lost in the nine days it took to control the flow.

Today, that much oil would be worth billions of dollars, but sometimes the laws of economics work in odd ways.

Before Spindletop blew, oil was worth $2 per barrel. With oil suddenly as plentiful as it appeared after the gusher began, the price dropped to $0.03 per barrel.

Of course, the price recovered, and by 1903 there were 400 oil-producing wells on Spindletop.

The University of Texas at Austin is the home for an extensive Oral History of the Texas Oil Industry. It began in 1951, when the wife of one of the original drillers of Spindletop worried that the stories about the early days of the Texas oil industry were at risk of being lost, the way much of the history of trail driving and railroading had been by then.

Recordings were made of the stories of those who had first-hand knowledge of "how it all began." Then, students indexed the transcripts to make them easier to use.

Much of the material is available to the public on site.

**T**he Hunt family name has a significant place in the economic history of Texas. In fact, it has several.

H.L. Hunt invested in a wildcat well in East Texas in the 1930s and made his fortune with the discovery of what became the largest oil field in the world at the time. When he died in 1974, his youngest son took over and expanded the business globally. Today, the Hunt Oil Company remains one of the largest privately held independent oil companies in the world.

eginning in 1973, two of H.L. Hunt's other sons decided they needed a hedge against inflation, so they started buying silver. Lots of it.

From 1973 to the start of 1979, the price of silver climbed from two to five dollars an ounce. That was when the brothers decided to actively pursue cornering the market. By early 1980, they, and their partners, owned more than half the world's supply and had driven the price as high as $54 an ounce.

A change in trading rules and some government intervention gradually brought the price down again, until on March 27, the market suffered a one-day drop of 50 percent (from $22 to $11).

The Hunt brothers wound up declaring bankruptcy and were convicted in 1988 of conspiring to manipulate the market.

Energy means more than oil in Texas. The state leads the United States in both natural gas production and the capacity to generate power from the wind.

In fact, Texas can produce more mega-watts of wind power than all but four other countries (aside from the United States)—Germany, China, Spain, and India.

Italy ranks next among nations, with just over half of the capacity of Texas alone.

Texans not only produce more electricity than any other state, they use more, too. And that's not just because the state is so big, either. The per capita residential use in Texas is higher than the national average.

Amarillo's Helium Monument was built in 1968 to mark the 100th anniversary of the discovery of the lighter-than-air gas and to designate that city as the Helium Capital of the World.

At the time, nearly all of Earth's helium supply was under U.S. government control and could be found within a few hundred miles of Amarillo. Much of the helium has now been moved, but the monument still stands, doing double- and triple-duty as a sundial and as a time capsule.

Each of the four columns in the 60-foot-high structure was stuffed with souvenirs of life in the Sixties. The last is to be opened after 1,000 years and is said to contain a savings account passbook originally worth $10. With interest, the account could hold $1 quadrillion by the time it's recovered.

**T**exas has more billionaires than any state other than New York and California, according to the 2010 Forbes list of rich people.

Of the 40 billionaires in the Lone Star state, most are from Dallas, but the richest live in Ft. Worth (Wal-Mart heiress Alice Walton) and Austin (Dell founder Michael Dell).

Dan L. Duncan, a Houstonian who ranked 74th on that list with $9 billion, died in spring 2010, becoming the first billionaire in U.S. history to pass his fortune to his heirs tax-free.

The United States unexpectedly allowed its estate tax to lapse at the end of 2009, for the first time since its inception in 1916. The tax is set to return at a higher rate in 2011. Meanwhile, those who die any time in between, like Duncan, do so free and clear.

Texas has no personal or corporate income tax or state property tax, and the overall tax burden on Texans is one of the lowest in the country.

There is a Gross Receipts Tax in Texas, amounting to an economy-wide tax on money/value changing hands.

Both local property and state sales taxes in Texas rank pretty high in comparison to other states.

In terms of federal taxes, Texas is a "donor state," meaning that Texas taxpayers pay in more than they get out.

The Lone Star state receives in federal funding about 94 cents of every tax dollar it sends to Washington.

Texas has the nation's highest share of workers earning at or less than the federal minimum wage.

Nationwide, more than 70 million people were paid by the hour in 2009, and about 5 percent of them earned minimum wage ($7.25/hour) or less.

Among Texans paid by the hour in the same year, more than 8 percent were at or below the minimum wage.

[Some earners are not covered by the minimum wage law—for example, full-time students, tipped employees, and student-learners are sometimes exempt.]

Eccentric millionaire Stanley Marsh 3—he finds the Roman numeral III too pretentious—is well-known in Amarillo for his outrageous art projects. The one that earned him national notoriety in the 1970s is the Cadillac Ranch.

As his monument to the American Dream, Marsh arranged to have 10 classic Cadillacs (1949–1963) planted nose-down in a field along Interstate 40. The trunks and tail-fins of these former gas guzzlers extend above ground, like whale flukes that become visible just before the big mammals dive.

Although Marsh had to move the art installation to stay clear of Amarillo's urban sprawl, Cadillac Ranch is still open to the public. In fact, visitors are encouraged to participate in the project by spray-painting graffiti on the rusted hulks.

nother roadside sculpture commissioned by Marsh was inspired by the work of British poet Percy Shelley. In his 1818 sonnet, *Ozymandias*, Shelley writes of "Two vast and trunkless legs of stone" that stand in the desert. In the Texas version, *Ozymandias* consists of two legs—one 24 feet high; the other, 34 feet—standing in a cow pasture along Interstate 27.

Like Marsh's Cadillac Ranch, this art project is subject to the occasional gratuitous paint job, and the feet have been seen adorned with sports socks.

arsh is also behind hundreds of bogus highway signs in Texas proclaiming surprise announcements (*e.g.*, "Road Does Not End") or posing questions (*e.g.*, "What is a village without village idiots?").

Marsh has been quoted as saying, "Art is a legalized form of insanity, and I do it very well."

irabeau B. Lamar became the second president of the Republic of Texas after a most unusual campaign.

Lamar's first opponent, Peter Grayson, had a history of mental illness and committed suicide.

Chief Justice James Collinsworth, the candidate who replaced Grayson, died after a week-long drinking binge when he either fell or jumped from a boat in Galveston with only a few days left in the race.

Lamar won by a huge margin.

While in office, President Lamar arranged the endowment of an educational system for Texas by setting aside public lands that, although worthless at the time, were ultimately quite valuable.

Today in Texas, the physical plants of the public higher education facilities alone are valued at $18 billion.

As a result, Lamar is called the "Father of Education in Texas."

About one-quarter of all Texans today age 25 and older have a bachelor's degree (or higher).

More than 55 percent of students that enter a Texas public institution of higher education earn their baccalaureate degree within six years.

In 2007, Texas public universities awarded more than 74,000 bachelor's degrees, 24,000 master's degrees, and 4,500 doctoral or professional degrees.

There is some evidence that the laws of probability do not apply in the state of Texas.

Anywhere else in the world, it might be impossible for anyone to win nearly $21 million by hitting the state lottery jackpot four separate times.

In Texas, however, Joan Ginther pulled it off by winning jackpots with three scratch-off tickets and one lottery draw.

The four-time winner, formerly of Bishop, Texas, has given no public statement on her methods. Or, for that matter, on *why* anyone who had already won *three* multimillion-dollar lotteries would continue buying tickets.

Maybe it's just luck, or maybe Dr. Ginther, who moved to Las Vegas, Nevada, actually knew what she was doing.

She is, after all, a math professor.

TEXAS
FACTS

Texas Instruments (TI) is the birthplace of the first integrated circuit, the backbone of today's computer culture.

By 1958, the transistor had already replaced the vacuum tube in electronics. Some applications were being built with thousands of transistors hand-wired together, which was terribly inefficient.

Jack Kilby was a new employee at TI that summer, so he didn't have any vacation time accrued when his colleagues went off for a summer break. And it was a lucky thing he didn't!

Kilby spent the time designing a circuit that could be built entirely out of a single block of silicon. His first working model was less than a half-inch long and was primitive by any standards, but it was enough to revolutionize the world of electronics.

exas-native Robert Dennard won the National Medal of Technology and was inducted into the National Inventors Hall of Fame for his contribution to the computer industry.

In 1968, while working for IBM, Dennard invented a memory chip capable of providing more memory at cheaper prices: the DRAM—Dynamic Random Access Memory.

Dr. Michael E. DeBakey spent the better part of his career in Houston reinventing the field of cardiovascular disease.

Dr. DeBakey's list of "firsts" is impressive—from establishing the surgical treatment of strokes, to repairing and bypassing cardiac arteries, to implanting artificial hearts—and barely begins to describe how he and his team at Baylor, throughout the second half of the 20th century, forged much of what has become modern-day medicine.

The list of health care facilities (*e.g.*, the Michael E. DeBakey Department of Surgery at Baylor College of Medicine) and inventions that bear his name (*e.g.*, the Micromed DeBakey VAD, a heart pump developed with NASA) are a testament to the impact of his work.

Mary Kay Ash of Hot Wells, Texas, was an executive in an era unfriendly to women in business. By the early 1960s, after being passed over for promotion yet again, she decided to create a paradigm shift for herself, and others like her, by creating a direct marketing company designed to resonate with the women that would become its sales force.

Today, Mary Kay Cosmetics is a global success by any measure—not just by the iconic pink Cadillacs awarded to top saleswomen.

A museum located in the company's world headquarters in Dallas secures its place in history. There, visitors can hear Mary Kay's motivational speeches and enter the Keepers of the Dream Independent National Sales Director Hall of Honor.

Admission is free, and tours of Mary Kay's office can be arranged in advance.

**T**exas can claim the first woman *elected* governor in the United States, but she wasn't the first woman to be governor. Miriam A. ("Ma") Ferguson was elected in 1924. She was *inaugurated* in 1925, two weeks *after* a woman became governor of Wyoming.

"Ma" Ferguson was married to former-Governor James E. Ferguson, who was barred from running again after he resigned in 1917, just before he could be removed from office on corruption charges.

Governor "Ma" Ferguson is remembered for having granted an average of 100 pardons a month during her first two-year term of office, which was also marred by charges of graft and corruption.

Although she lost bids for re-election in 1926 and 1930, she served again from 1933 to 1935, when she fought the Depression with loans for cotton farmers and "bread bonds" to feed starving children.

One of Governor "Ma" Ferguson's many full pardons went to "Buck" Barrow, who quickly took advantage of being released from prison to continue a life of crime. Buck and his wife got together with Buck's brother, Clyde, and his girlfriend Bonnie Parker, who were already notorious criminals.

A few months later, in a shootout with police, Buck was killed, and his wife Blanche was captured. Bonnie and Clyde continued their crime spree.

onnie Parker and Clyde Barrow were both Texas natives. They met in Dallas in 1930 and formed a criminal partnership that included jailbreaks, robberies, kidnappings, and murders.

Their crime-spree prompted a well-publicized nationwide manhunt that ended on May 23, 1934, when a group of lawmen ambushed the couple and killed them.

Since then, their short careers as law-breakers have been popularized in films and songs, and the Texas Rangers Museum in Waco has a display of exhibits related to their ultimate demise.

When a fairly mundane property case involving a fraternal association called the Woodmen of the World (WOW) was appealed to the Texas Supreme Court in 1924, it caused a problem. All three justices were members of WOW and could not rule on the case.

After 10 months of searching, the governor could find no one qualified to serve that was not also a member of WOW.

Of course, he wasn't looking in the right place. Women couldn't join WOW, but they could be Supreme Court Justices, as long as they were attorneys that met the qualifications.

So Hattie Henenberg, Hortense Ward, and Ruth Brazzil were appointed and served for five months as the first ever all-female Supreme Court.

For the record, the women ruled in favor of WOW.

exas is one of only two states (Oklahoma is the other) that has two "supreme" courts: one for civil cases and one for criminal cases.

The split dates back to the 1870s, when the court that is now the Criminal Court of Appeals was created. Each year the nine judges and a staff of 60 people handle more than 12,000 criminal legal matters—from routine appeals to death penalty cases.

Decisions of the Criminal Court of Appeals are final. The Texas Supreme Court doesn't get to review those, but its nine justices have more than enough to do. That Court is responsible for the administration of the entire judicial system in the state, including sole authority over who gets to be a lawyer.

Texas appears consistently at the top of the list when it comes to the death penalty.

Since executions resumed in the United States in 1976, Texas has executed more than four times as many people as the next state on the list, Virginia.

Forty people were executed in Texas in 2000.

In 2007, executions in the state accounted for 60 percent of the death sentences carried out nationally.

There were more than 300 inmates on death row in Texas at the beginning of 2010.

Huntsville is the home of the oldest state prison in Texas, opened in 1849. The Walls Unit, as the prison is known, held "Old Sparky," the electric chair built by inmates when electrocution was authorized to replace hanging as the mode of execution in the state.

"Old Sparky" was the last stop for more than 360 inmates from 1924 to 1964. Today, the chair rests in the Capital Punishment Exhibit of the Texas Prison Museum a few miles from the Walls Unit.

The museum also has a contraband exhibit of ingeniously hidden weapons and a collection of inmate art.

As a public service, the Prison Museum will research the convict ledgers for a $10 fee per convict. Information available from the ledgers includes the basics—name, number, body markings, etc.

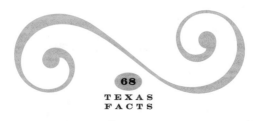

Robert and Elizabeth Barrett Browning, the well-known English poets, were a mainstay of Victorian literature. Naturally, then, one would find the world's largest collection of books, letters, manuscripts, and memorabilia pertaining to the Brownings in...Texas?

When the couple's son died in 1912, his entire collection of his parents' work and estate were sold at auction in London. Shortly thereafter, Andrew Joseph Armstrong of Baylor University in Waco began his quest of tracking down and reuniting as much of the collection as possible.

Today, Baylor's Armstrong Browning Library has its own building and a growing collection of materials that entitle it to be the "library of record" for the Brownings' work.

No need to travel outside Texas to enjoy the best in Spanish art. One of the largest and most comprehensive collections outside of Spain can be found in the Meadows Museum at Southern Methodist University (SMU).

The idea of bringing a thousand years of Spanish heritage to the Dallas/Ft. Worth area came to Texas philanthropist and oil financier Algur H. Meadows in the 1950s, when he was making frequent business trips to Spain. Meadows was so impressed by the artwork he saw there that he decided to build a "small Prado in Texas."

Today, the collection includes masterworks by Velazquez, Goya, Murillo, Ribera, Miro, and Picasso, as well as complete first editions of Goya's four print series.

The Buckhorn Saloon and Museum in San Antonio is filled with Texas oddities and paraphernalia.

First opened in 1881, the saloon catered to a clientele that didn't always have enough money to pay the check. So the owner started accepting horns and antlers. The owner's wife took jars of rattlesnake rattles. A museum adjunct was inevitable.

Today, the collection includes a world-record whitetail deer called the 78-Point Buck, a 10,000-year-old Irish elk skull and antlers, and longhorns that measure more than eight feet across.

The saloon recently added a second museum honoring the lawmen of the Texas Rangers, including a re-creation of San Antonio at the turn of the century, and a Bonnie and Clyde exhibit.

Hundreds of Native American tribes lived in the land that became Texas when Europeans first "discovered" it.

Some of those tribes wound up giving their names to U.S. states and cities: Alabama and Delaware; Biloxi, Cheyenne, Waco, and Wichita.

Among the other large tribes in Texas were the Apache, the Comanche, the Caddo, the Chickasaw, the Coahuiltecan, the Kiowa, the Kickapoo, the Arapaho, the Shawnee, and the Cherokee.

The Mound Builder culture was prominent in North America for more than 2,000 years before the arrival of the Europeans, and the remains of their southwestern-most ceremonial center is near present-day Nacogdoches.

Built about 1,200 years ago by a group of Caddo Indians known as the Hasinai, the mounds still visible today were used for burials and religious ceremonies.

The word "Texas" is not Spanish.

It comes from the language of the Hasinai and translates roughly to "Greetings, Friend."

Or perhaps, a more accurate Texan translation would be, "Howdy, Pardner."

The Pueblo Indians have one of three recognized Native American reservations in Texas. The Tigua Tribal Council of Ysleta del Sur Pueblo is the oldest government in the state. The Tiguas founded the Ysleta Mission in 1682 and were given a land grant by the Spanish government in Mexico.

When Texas became a state, the government did not recognize the land grant and gradually took the land away. In 1968, the state of Texas recognized the Tigua as a tribe and the federal government established their land as a reservation.

Today, a tribal population of about 1,200 lives in Ysleta del Sur Pueblo.

The Kickapoo Traditional Tribe of Texas are Woodlands Indians that speak an Algonquin language. They were not originally from the area, but their dealings with Europeans and with other tribes gradually forced them south to where they live today.

The tribe was officially recognized by the U.S. government in 1983.

The Kickapoo reservation in Texas is on the border with Mexico, adjacent to the land occupied by the Mexican Kickapoos. The U.S. side has a population of fewer than 500 people.

The tribe owns and operates the Lucky Eagle casino near Eagle Pass.

The Alabama-Coushatta Tribe of Texas has the oldest reservation in the state, located in the Big Thicket.

The Alabama and the Coushatta began as two separate, but related, tribes, after the Republic of Texas promised each tribe a parcel of land, but only followed through with a grant of one.

More than 100 years later, after receiving assistance from the state and federal governments, the Alabama-Coushatta tribe began to establish self-governance with the creation of a Tribal Council.

In 1987, federal legislation granted official recognition to the Alabama-Coushatta.

**T**wo U.S. presidents were born in Texas—and neither of them was named Bush.

Dwight David Eisenhower was the first, born in Denison in 1890 and elected as the 34th president in 1952.

Lyndon Baines Johnson, born in Stonewall in 1908, became the 36th president in 1963, upon the assassination of John F. Kennedy.

The Bushes were both born in New England.

Sandra Day O'Connor, born in El Paso, became the first woman to serve on the U.S. Supreme Court in 1981.

Her journey is a testament to the changing role of women in society during her lifetime. When she graduated third in her class at Stanford Law School in 1952, she had trouble finding a job because law firms weren't hiring women.

She retired from the Court in 2005 and turned her efforts toward encouraging civic education and involvement. She has been the driving force behind such projects for children as ourcourts.org and iCivics.org.

After the Civil War, for the first time, black men could join the U.S. Army in peace-time. The military offered many men a chance for a better life, and many blacks, including former slaves and wartime veterans, signed up for the opportunity.

Called "Buffalo Soldiers," the blacks that served in the U.S. Army in Texas earned a reputation for fierce fighting, relentless determination, and solid discipline. In addition to combat, they also provided protective escort services to wagon trains and other civilian groups.

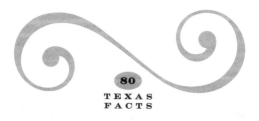

Six different national flags have flown over Texas since Spanish explorers first "claimed" it in 1519.

For a short period, from 1685 to 1690, Texas was a French territory before reverting to Spain.

Texas was part of Mexico when that country won its independence from Spain in 1821.

Texas adopted its own Declaration of Independence in 1836 and became a separate republic after a brief war with Mexico.

In 1845, the United States annexed Texas, making it the 28th state until it seceded to become part of the Confederate States of America.

Texas was readmitted to the United States after the Civil War in 1870.

So, the six flags of Texas belonged to Spain, France, Mexico, Texas, the United States, and the Confederacy.

The Texas State Nickname is "The Lone Star State," and the Texas flag has, appropriately, a lone white star on a red, white, and blue flag.

So there can be no misinterpretation, the Legislature has spelled out the symbolism of each of those colors:

- Red is for bravery.
- White is for purity.
- Blue is for loyalty.

The ethnic mix of settlers in Texas, going back hundreds of years, is so extensive there's a museum dedicated to celebrating it.

The Institute of Texan Cultures is part of the University of Texas at San Antonio, and it is affiliated with the Smithsonian Institution. The huge complex houses exhibits, programs, special events, and interactive displays on *all* the groups that combine to form the history of the Lone Star state—and there are a *lot* of them.

The *Texans One and All* exhibit showcases more than 20 of the ethnic groups that originally settled in Texas, with interactive displays that tell their stories and provide examples of their experiences. And *Living Texas* gives visitors an interpretive first-hand experience of what life was like in days gone by.

TEXAS
FACTS

The town of White Settlement, near Fort Worth, got its name in the 1850s to distinguish it from the nearby settlement of Native Americans. The city was incorporated in 1941. In 2005, the citizens of White Settlement voted, by a margin of nearly 11-to-1, to keep the status quo rather than change the city name to West Settlement.

During World War II, Crystal City, Texas, was the home of the nation's largest Alien Family Internment Camp. Operated by the federal Justice Department from 1942 through 1947, the camp housed German, Italian, and Japanese families. With more than 500 buildings on 290 acres, the camp held almost 4,000 people.

The camp also held Peruvians of Japanese descent who were brought to the United States for a potential future exchange of U.S. civilians with Japan. When the war was over, Peru refused to repatriate the Japanese Latin Americans. Many were sent to Japan; some remained in Texas, but they were not allowed to begin pursuing U.S. citizenship until the 1950s.

visitor from Bhutan might feel very much at home at the University of Texas at El Paso (UTEP).

When a fire destroyed the School of Mines and Metallurgy in 1917, the new buildings were modeled after pictures the dean's wife had seen in a National Geographic article about the tiny Himalayan kingdom a few years earlier.

Over the years, the school became part of UTEP, and the link between the campus and Bhutan grew.

When the Prince visited UTEP for its 2008 Bhutan Festival, he strengthened the ties with the donation of an actual Bhutanese temple. Originally built in the Himalayas for a Smithsonian folklife festival in Washington, D.C., the 30-foot temple was eventually relocated to El Paso, to the school that refers to itself as "Bhutan on the Border."

The Czech-American population in Texas, one of the largest in the United States today, traces its roots as far back as the Republic itself.

Within a month of his arrival in 1836, the first Czech immigrant joined the Texas army to fight Mexico. He played the fife at the Battle of San Jacinto, the decisive battle of the Revolution.

zech immigration began in earnest in the 1850s, and by the 1900s there were 250 Czech settlements in Texas, mostly on the Blackland Prairie.

Today, the handiwork of those early settlers can still be seen in the beautiful Painted Churches of Texas. Local artists used bright colors to decorate the interiors of these Catholic houses of worship to remind them of home.

More than two dozen Painted Churches in Texas are on the National Register of Historic Sites.

I f it's the Friday before the first Monday in November (got that?), it's time for Wurstfest! This weeklong homage to sausage, beer, and all things German has been going on in New Braunfels for more than half a century. It owes its roots to Prince Carl von Solms-Braunfels and the thousands of German immigrants that followed him to bring a piece of the Fatherland to North America.

The Prince established New Braunfels in 1845. The next year, as the wave of Teutonic immigration continued, another colony was established at Fredericksburg. By 1850, Germans accounted for 5 percent of the entire population of Texas. By 1880, one-third of the residents of San Antonio were German.

Although the German-language press in Texas died out in the 1950s, the local paper is still the *Herald-Zeitung*.

Perhaps the most famous "sailor man" in the world—Popeye—made his first appearance in Texas.

Popeye started his career in a comic strip called "Thimble Theatre," which appeared first in the Victoria *Advocate*.

he Victoria *Advocate* started life as a weekly in 1846, within six months of the annexation of Texas as a U.S. state. An *extra* edition was published the same day the newspaper premiered to announce the Battle of Palo Alto, which marked the start of the Mexican War.

The paper became the *Daily Advocate* in 1897 and it is still published as a daily paper today. In fact, the *Advocate* boasts that it "missed publication only a few times because of fires in 1876 and 1892, and the Civil War, when it could not publish due to lack of newsprint."

Everyone knows the Civil War ended with the surrender of Robert E. Lee to Ulysses S. Grant at Appomattox, Virginia, in April 1865. Except, it didn't.

The last battle of the Civil War took place more than a month later, just outside Brownsville, Texas. The soldiers on both sides were aware that the South had already capitulated, but the Confederate soldiers were not yet prepared to yield.

The Battle of Palmito Ranch was a victory, of sorts, for an outnumbered but determined group of rebels from the Texan cavalry.

The fighting went on for about four hours, with the Union soldiers retreating and the Texans in hot pursuit. In the end, only a few dozen Confederates were wounded, but more than 100 federal soldiers had died.

A truce was established a few days later.

When Union troops arrived in Galveston on June 19, 1865, the message they carried stunned many in the crowd that greeted them. Not only was the Civil War over, but all slaves were now free.

To be sure there was no misunderstanding, the announcement continued: "This involves an absolute equality of personal rights and rights of property between former masters and slaves, and the connection heretofore existing between them becomes that between employer and hired labor."

The day came to be known as *Juneteenth*, and it has been celebrated ever since.

Because it was sometimes hard to find a place where celebrations could be held, many ex-slaves purchased land to serve as "emancipation grounds" for large public gatherings, like Emancipation Park in Houston, purchased in 1872.

Juneteenth became an official Texas state holiday in 1980.

June 20th is officially Audie Murphy Day in Texas. During WWII, the Texas native earned every decoration of valor the United States had to offer, plus five more from France and Belgium, for a total of 33.

After the war, Murphy launched a 25-year career as an actor, making 44 feature films. He was also a hit songwriter, and his autobiography, *To Hell and Back*, was a best-seller. When the book was made into a movie, Murphy starred as himself.

During the Korean War, Murphy joined the Texas National Guard. He was in the U.S. Army Reserve until his death in 1971, at the age of 46, in a plane crash.

Murphy is honored with a memorial in Farmersville, a statue in San Antonio, and a collection in the Texas Heritage Museum at Hill College.

TEXAS
FACTS

Today, the spiciest thing found at the State Fair of Texas is probably the chili, but it used to be the sideshows.

Peep shows and dancing girls were commonplace at the Fairs beginning in the late 1800s and continuing through to the middle of the 20th century.

One popular attraction in 1936, for example, was Corinne, the Apple Dancer. Her billing was a description of her wardrobe, which, in addition to a g-string, consisted of a ball about the size of an apple.

The next year, famed stripper Gypsy Rose Lee was a performer at the fair.

The Fort Worth Frontier Centennial in 1936 included a headline act by Sally Rand, whose claim to fame was a fan-dance that showed little but sparked the imagination. What she brought with her to Texas, however, was a bit more explicit: Sally Rand's Nude Ranch. (Get it? "Nude" instead of "Dude"!)

The "ranch" consisted of little more than scantily clad girls lounging, playing ball, riding horses, and shooting bows and arrows.

Rand was well-received. In fact, November 6, 1936, was designated "Sally Rand Day" by the city, as a tribute and a way to show gratitude for her "artistry" and for the "culture and progress" she brought with her to town.

*Sufferin' succotash*, Daffy Duck has Texas in his blood!

Tex Avery, an animator born in Taylor, is credited with creating the iconic cartoon character during his tenure with Warner Brothers.

Tex Avery is said to have been a descendent of both Daniel Boone and Judge Roy Bean.

Judge Roy Bean was a legendary Justice of the Peace in Langtry, Texas, in the late 1800s. Bean owned and operated the Jersey Lilly, a saloon from which he would dispense his own brand of justice. He was known for his creative interpretations of the law and the unusual sentences he imposed.

One story describes how, when Bean learned that a dead accident victim had a gun and $40 in his pockets, he fined the corpse exactly $40 for carrying a concealed weapon and confiscated the gun. He used the money to buy a casket and a headstone and to pay the gravedigger. (He kept the gun.)

The bad news is that Tyson Turk, a body-piercing artist in Arlington, did not achieve his goal of poking 2,000 holes in Jeremy Stroud, a diesel mechanic, in 2009.

Although Stroud had volunteered for the job, his stamina gave out at 1,197.

The good news is that the previous record for body piercings in a single sitting was only 900, so Turk managed to break the record.

The odd news, if in fact this story is not odd enough, is that the previous record was also held by Turk.

TEXAS
FACTS

Stephen F. Austin is called the "father of Texas" because he launched the first Anglo-American settlement of Texas under an 1821 grant from the Mexican government.

He was given permission to build a colony of 300 families in southeast Texas.

The majority of the "Old Three Hundred," as those families are now called, were from the upper classes of the American southeast— Louisiana, Alabama, Arkansas, Tennessee, and Missouri. Many of them came with their slaves and built plantations that prospered.

By 1836, at the beginning of the Texas War for Independence, 35,000 to 50,000 people had settled in Texas.

If a Texan says, "Come and take it," it's not an invitation. It's a dare!

The phrase dates back to the first military engagement in the Texas struggle for independence.

The Mexican government had loaned a cannon to the town of Gonzales, to defend against Indian attacks. The cannon didn't really work, but it made noise and was therefore effective.

In 1835, the military demanded the cannon back. When the army came to retrieve it, the Texans raised a flag painted with a single star, a drawing of the weapon, and the words "Come and Take It."

The Mexican force retreated to San Antonio empty-handed after a brief exchange of fire, including one blast from the harmless cannon. That cannon volley came to be known as the "Texan Shot Heard Round the World."

The Texas Declaration of Independence was presented to the Convention of 1836 on March 2, at Washington-on-the-Brazos. After it was signed, the document was sent to a printer with an order for five hand-written copies and 1,000 printed copies. The original was sent to the U.S. State Department in Washington, D.C.

None of the hand-written copies and only 12 of the printed ones are known to exist today. The original was returned to Texas in the 1890s.

About 25 copies of the original printing of the U.S. Declaration of Independence are still around today. The only one in the western United States is on permanent display at the Dallas Public Library.

Another treasure in that library's collection is one of the remaining 250 copies of the first edition of Shakespeare's plays, known as the "First Folio" and printed in 1623.

Remember the Alamo?

The famous fort started life in 1718 as a Franciscan mission, San Antonio de Valero. The goal was to convert the local Coahuiltecan Indians to Christianity, but raids by the neighboring Comanches and Apaches ultimately proved too much for the friars.

In 1794, the mission became a military installation known as the Alamo.

At the beginning of the 20th century, the Alamo had fallen into disrepair and was on the verge of being converted into a hotel.

Clara Driscoll, a young heiress whose travels to Europe had given her an appreciation for the importance of protecting historic places, stepped forward to rescue the property.

Working with the Daughters of the Republic of Texas, Driscoll used her own funds to purchase the Alamo to save it for posterity, winning her the honorary title of "Savior of the Alamo."

In 1836, when Texas declared its independence, Mexican dictator Santa Anna led thousands of troops to put down the rebellion.

First stop—the Alamo, where a small band of Texans were killed after a 13-day siege.

Among them were such famous names as Davy Crockett and Jim Bowie.

Crockett had represented Tennessee in the U.S. Congress. When he ran for his third term, he told his constituents he would represent them faithfully if re-elected, and if not, "You may all go to hell and I will go to Texas." He lost. . .and went to Texas.

Bowie was a Texas Ranger whose knife-fighting skills brought him fame. In fact, the kind of hunting knife he used is named after him—the Bowie knife.

As the story goes, when the situation at the Alamo was obviously hopeless, Lt. Col. William Barrett Travis drew his sword and scratched a line in the dirt, inviting those willing to die to cross it and join him.

Only one man replied, "No, thanks."

Louis Moses Rose had proven his bravery time and again, as a veteran serving with Napoleon in France and with Jim Bowie in Texas. When it came to facing certain death, though, Rose drew his own line, choosing life over death.

Rose left the Alamo under cover of darkness and made his way through enemy lines, surviving only to find scorn and rejection from Texans who called him a coward.

Rose spent the rest of his life testifying on behalf of heirs of Alamo martyrs looking to Texas for compensation.

**W**eeks after the siege at the Alamo, a Mexican general captured about 350 Texans at Goliad. They were held at Presidio de la Bahia—which has been restored and is open to tourists today—until Santa Anna ordered them executed.

The Mexicans told the Texans they were being transported to another facility and marched them out on the road, single-file. Each prisoner had a Mexican guard to his left. On cue, the guards all killed their assigned prisoners.

"Remember the Alamo!" and "Remember Goliad!" became rallying cries at the next meeting of the two armies, the Battle of San Jacinto, where the war ended.

Santa Anna pursued a retreating Texas army to the San Jacinto River. Believing he had Sam Houston's forces cornered, he established his position and awaited reinforcements.

Both sides were encamped within a thousand yards of each other, on a three-square-mile piece of land completely surrounded by flood waters. Confident of his position, Santa Anna allowed his forces to rest before the final assault.

Meanwhile, Houston decided not to wait to be attacked, and Santa Anna made one fatal flaw: he didn't post sentries around the camp during the afternoon siesta.

Houston ordered the only bridge off the island destroyed, then led his forces in a very successful sneak attack.

The actual battle took only 18 minutes. Nine Texans and 700 Mexicans died. More than 730 Mexicans were captured, and the war was effectively over.

egend has it that one other strategic error cost Santa Anna the war.

Emily West was a slave belonging to a Texan who owned property in the area.

On the eve of the Battle of San Jacinto, Santa Anna captured Emily, who is said to have seduced the General by plying him with food and champagne on the day he had set aside for rest before battle.

Her selfless act was enough of a distraction to allow Houston and his men to sneak up on the Mexican camp and rule the day.

The story of Emily's sacrifice is immortalized in the lyrics to the song *The Yellow Rose of Texas*.

With the Battle of San Jacinto and the defeat of Santa Anna's army, nearly a million square miles of territory effectively changed sovereignty.

The site is a National Historic Landmark today, consisting of the battleground, a memorial, and the battleship *Texas*.

At 570 feet, with a 34-foot star on top, the monument is the tallest stone column memorial structure in the world. It is 15 feet taller than the Washington Monument in Washington, D.C.

An elevator brings visitors to an observation floor 489 feet above the battleground.

The *Texas*, permanently anchored on the Buffalo Bayou, is the first battleship memorial museum in the United States. It was presented to the state of Texas and commissioned as the flagship of the Texas Navy on the anniversary of Texas Independence in 1948.

**E**very state has a branch of the National Guard, but only Texas has its own navy. In fact, it's on its *third*.

The first Texas Navy was launched in 1836 with five ships, but all were lost by the middle of the following year.

The second Texas Navy was commissioned in 1839, but didn't fair much better. Economic difficulties and the ultimate annexation of Texas by the United States ended all traces of the second navy by 1857.

The third Texas Navy was established in the early 1970s as a nonprofit organization to preserve the naval history of the Republic of Texas.

The Texas Rangers is the oldest law enforcement agency with statewide jurisdiction in the United States, having been established by Stephen F. Austin, the Father of Texas, in 1823 to protect the Old Three Hundred he brought to colonize the region.

The Rangers were reauthorized by the Texas Republic and grew into a well-respected, elite fighting force. Combining guerilla tactics and the most sophisticated weapon of the time, the Colt revolver, the Rangers developed a reputation for getting the job done.

Today, there are 144 Rangers that serve as an investigative division of the Texas Department of Public Safety.

The Republic of Texas maintained diplomatic relations with France from 1836 until annexation in 1845.

Both countries built a legation (a form of embassy) in the other's capital city.

The Texas Legation in Paris was located where the Hotel de Vendome is today.

In Austin, the former French Legation is now a museum. The two-story Louisiana Bayou-style building is one of the only structures remaining in Austin from the days of the Texas Republic.

England never formally recognized the Republic of Texas, because it didn't want to upset Mexico.

The two countries did, however, establish a treaty that provided for commerce between them.

A Texas Legation was established in London, in offices rented just a few yards from St. James Palace. The building is still there today. In fact, the company from which Texas rented the space is still in business in the same location: Berry Bros. & Rudd's London Wine Shop at 3 St. James's Street.

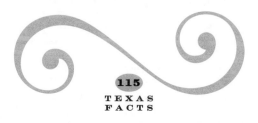

on't believe everything you read about Texas!

"Texas was the only U.S. state admitted by treaty" is a claim often seen on lists about the Lone Star state, but it isn't true.

Although a treaty was negotiated between the Republic of Texas and U.S. President John Tyler in April 1844, it was overwhelmingly defeated by the U.S. Senate for a number of political reasons, including anti-slavery sentiment and fears of war with Mexico.

A Joint Resolution approving annexation of Texas was passed by the U.S. Congress in 1845 and served as the basis for the admission of Texas as a state.

As part of the deal, Congress said that Texas could carve as many as four additional states out of its territory, at its "convenience," and those states would also be admitted to the union.

As a legal matter, it is not clear whether the secession of Texas and its readmission as a state after the Civil War has nullified that option.

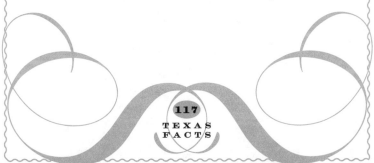

"**H**onor the Texas flag; I pledge allegiance to thee, Texas, one state under God, one and indivisible."

Texas has had a pledge of allegiance since 1933.

Since 2003, Texas students have been required to say both the U.S. and the state pledge once a day, as well as to observe a moment of silence. (Parents who object can exempt their children by sending a note to school.)

The phrase "one state under God" was added in 2007.

Sam Houston, the hero of San Jacinto, went on to become the President of the Republic of Texas (twice) and the Governor of the State of Texas. (He was also the Governor of Tennessee before all of that happened, a double-header that no one else can claim.)

Today, Houston's figure towers over Huntsville, as the "world's largest statue of an American hero," at 67 feet on a 10-foot base.

Founded in 1836, the City of Houston has a population of 1.9 million, making it the largest city in Texas (by population) and the fourth-largest in the United States, behind New York, Los Angeles, and Chicago.

The Port of Houston is the nation's largest port if measured by international tonnage. It comes in second for total tonnage.

The Houston Livestock Show and Rodeo, the world's largest, attracts nearly 2 million visitors each year.

The first word spoken to Earth by a human on the surface of the moon was "Houston," in 1969.

The stage for that moment was set in September 1961, when NASA announced its Space Task Group would move to Texas to establish the new Manned Spacecraft Center (MSC).

Houston was chosen from among 23 locations that fit a NASA list of criteria that included a mild climate, barge transportation in ice-free water, a nearby university, and lots of cheap land.

Of course, it also helped that both the Speaker of the House (Sam Rayburn) and the Vice President of the United States (Lyndon Johnson) were from Texas.

The U.S. Senate passed a resolution to rename the MSC after Johnson less than a month after his death. It became the JSC on February 17, 1973.

Almost everyone who has been to outer space has, at one time or another, lived in Houston.

It wasn't until June 2010, however, that someone who was actually *born* in Houston made it into orbit.

Dr. Shannon Walker served as flight engineer on the Russian Soyuz mission that began her six-month residence aboard the International Space Station.

David Wolf was the first American to vote from space.

The U.S. astronaut was aboard the Russian space station Mir on election day in 1997, the same year Texas made it possible for orbiting citizens to cast their ballots.

It wasn't exactly a secret ballot, though.

Dr. Wolf voted by e-mail through U.S. flight controllers in Moscow.

There were more than 30 issues included on the ballot that year, and his votes were read by an election official on the ground and entered by hand.

The technology has been used since then to allow astronauts on the International Space Station to perform their civic duty.

About 25,000 years ago, Texas was attacked by a swarm of nickel-iron meteors. The evidence remains just outside Odessa, where one of the three largest meteorite craters in the world can be found.

Hundreds of pounds of extraterrestrial rock fragments have been recovered from the site, which is 500 to 650 feet wide, from rim to rim.

The depth of the crater, though, was only about 100 feet when first formed, and after millennia of natural weathering, the deepest point is barely 15 feet today. That's why nothing special about the area was even noticed until 1892.

It took another three decades for anyone to realize that "it came from outer space," and a visitor center wasn't built until the turn of the 21st century.

But now, the Odessa craters are open for business.

**B**alcones Escarpment is Texas' fault. This isn't a blame game. It's a geological fact.

An *escarpment* is a ridge or cliff formed along a fault line in the earth's crust.

This fault is not particularly active, so the danger of a major earthquake in the region is pretty slim.

The Balcones Escarpment simply marks the difference between the low, flat eastern plains and the more rugged and slightly higher terrain to the west of the fault line that runs through or near Austin, San Marcos, San Antonio, and Waco.

**A**udrey, Claudette, Rita, Humberto, Ike... to name just a few of the hurricanes that have plagued Galveston.

The worst came without warning in 1900, before hurricanes even had names. The low-lying island was completely submerged by the storm surge, leaving an estimated 8,000 people dead and another 10,000 homeless—the worst natural disaster in U.S. history.

The city later built a seawall that protected life and property during the 1915 hurricane, but the beaches that lay outside the wall were completely swept away.

On average, the city of Galveston is affected by a hurricane every three years and is hit directly every nine!

Galveston's unfortunate vulnerability to destructive weather forces overshadowed its excellent location as a seaport, ruining any chance the city had of fulfilling its original economic promise of becoming the "New York of the South."

The first Neiman Marcus Store opened in Dallas in 1907 using $25,000 in seed money.

Herbert Marcus, his sister Carrie Marcus Neiman, and her husband Al Neiman were partners with experience in retailing and a desire to hit it big.

That was why they turned down the opportunity to purchase the Kansas-Missouri franchise for some unknown soda called Coca-Cola.

As it turned out, they did okay anyway, with a specialty store that caters to a well-heeled clientele, offering luxurious and one-of-a-kind items through its signature Christmas catalogue.

Today, Neiman Marcus is a chain that also owns, among other things, the Bergdorf Goodman name.

In addition to stores throughout the country, the chain makes its goods available on the Internet.

In the heart of Dallas, alongside the Convention Center, a cattle drive has been captured in bronze to honor the role cowboys played in the city's history.

Pioneer Plaza is the largest public open space in the business district, and it's full of larger-than-life sculptures of longhorns and cowhands moving them along the trail.

The adjacent Pioneer Cemetery contains a large Civil War Memorial featuring Confederate heroes Robert E. Lee, Stonewall Jackson, and Jefferson Davis.

George Bannerman Dealey moved to Texas from England as a child with his family in 1870. He took a job as an office boy with the *Galveston News* in 1874, and ultimately owned the company when it published the *Dallas Morning News*.

Dealey launched WFAA radio, helped establish Southern Methodist University, brought a Federal Reserve Bank to Dallas, and was a director of the Children's Hospital.

One of the most popular Dallas landmarks, Dealey Plaza, was named for him because of his efforts to clean up the city.

But the well-known tourist attraction isn't visited today because of the good works of its namesake.

This world-famous location is visited by millions annually because it is where President John F. Kennedy was assassinated in 1963.

TEXAS
FACTS

The "Wade" of the historic 1973 Supreme Court abortion decision, *Roe v. Wade*, was Henry Menasco Wade, district attorney of Dallas County.

Wade had been in the national spotlight in 1963, as the official who first publicly declared that Lee Harvey Oswald was the lone gunman responsible for killing President John F. Kennedy, then again as the prosecutor of Jack Ruby for the murder of Oswald.

Although Wade had not actually handled the abortion case that made its way to the Supreme Court, he was listed in the case name as the respondent because he was the lawyer in charge of law enforcement for the jurisdiction.

**131**

TEXAS
FACTS

In 1961, the Dallas city planners decided to dedicate an acre of land to a "value."

Then came the hard part: which "value" should be so honored? And which acre of land should be set aside for that purpose?

Fifteen years later, the Chapel of Thanksgiving was opened at Thanks-Giving Square in Dallas.

With "gratitude" as its central theme, the chapel is packed with international symbols of thanks—including giant church bells forged in France, a meditation garden, 15-ton monoliths of white Sierra granite, a 7,000-pound altar that is a cube of Carrera marble, and a 60-foot-high stained-glass installation called the Glory Window.

In 1996, Thanks-Giving Square expanded from one acre to more than three.

Its interfaith mission traces its roots to expressions of gratitude found in all the world's cultures and religions.

Texas has two entries in the First Thanksgiving in the New World sweepstakes.

Spanish explorer Francisco Vasquez de Coronado got very lost in 1541 leading an expedition of 1,500 men in search of the mythical riches of the Seven Cities of Cibola.

He arrived, instead, at Palo Duro Canyon, where a plentiful supply of water and fruit prompted the grateful explorer to oversee a Thanksgiving celebration.

In spring of 1598, Juan de Onate was another Spanish expedition leader who nearly led his followers to their death, crossing the Chihuahuan Desert from Mexico in search of their place in history. The food and water supply were gone five days before the end of their 50-day march to the Rio Grande, but the group made it...and gave thanks decades before those copy-cat Pilgrims in New England.

The San Antonio River has a history of flooding.

In 1921, a flash flood put nine feet of water in the streets, killing 50 people.

That prompted the design of a bypass channel to straighten the river and control the water. (That would teach it!)

After years of give-and-take between city planners and conservationists, a plan was approved for a River Walk.

Walkways, stairways to street level, footbridges, and rock walls lining the banks all combined to capitalize on the beauty of the river, while minimizing the risk of flooding.

In the 1960s, the designers of Disneyland recommended emphasizing the colonial history of the region to increase the commercial value of the River Walk, which became the *Paseo del Rio*—a central attraction of San Antonio today.

In addition to the shops and restaurants that attract people to San Antonio's *Paseo del Rio* daily, the three-mile-long promenade is the site for a nearly continuous series of festivals and parades.

One of the most recent additions to the calendar is the Lucky Duck Race and Festival, in which 20,000 rubber ducks are dropped into the river and "race" to a finish line downstream.

Each rubber duck is "adopted" by a donor who stands to earn a prize if the surrogate waterfowl "wins."

The event to support both the River Walk and a local homeless shelter began in 2010 and is intended to continue annually.

The most famous brothel in the world, the Chicken Ranch, was a fixture in La Grange for more than 130 years, until 1973.

The house of prostitution got its name during the Depression, when patrons are said to have traded chickens for sex. (Given the economy, a steady supply of food was considered pretty good income.)

The end came when a Houston TV reporter publicized the existence of the brothel, which previously had been a well-known secret, and demonized the enterprise.

All that exists of the entire episode today is the prominent mention of the Chicken Ranch on the La Grange city website and the worldwide popularity of the musical and movie *The Best Little Whorehouse in Texas*, which retells the story.

The FBI named El Paso and Austin two of the safest big U.S. cities in 2009, saying they had the third and fourth lowest crime rates in the country, respectively.

exas cities may be booming, but they haven't taken over yet!

More than 80 percent of the land in Texas is still rural, and about 14 percent of the total population—or a little more than three million people—live there.

For perspective, the population of rural Texas is greater than the combined populations of Alaska, North Dakota, Vermont, Wyoming, and the District of Columbia.

The Texas State instrument is the guitar, and few in history have done more to change the world of music with it than Lubbock's native-son Buddy Holly.

Today, the city remembers the legend and his immeasurable influence on rock and roll with the Buddy Holly Center.

Holly's music, including his enduring hits like "That'll Be the Day" and "Peggy Sue," continues to speak for itself. Combining music and visual arts into interactive and dynamic exhibits, the Center ensures that the determination and commitment of the man to his craft is remembered as well.

One recent addition to the Center's collection is furniture from Holly's boyhood home, including the mattress, box spring, headboard, dresser, and mirror he used as a teenager.

The Armadillo World Headquarters (AWHQ) lasted for 10 years as a music venue in Austin, where some of the most recognizable names in music came to play: Count Basie, the Ramones, Robert Palmer, Frank Zappa, and Talking Heads.

Working on a shoestring, local musicians rented and remodeled a former National Guard armory and turned it into a "happening." With room for 1,500 people (as long as they sat on the floor), the AWHQ gave musical greats like Marcia Ball and Stevie Ray Vaugan some of their earliest exposure.

Texas native Willie Nelson returned from Nashville in 1972 to lead the evolution of a whole new sub-genre of country music.

Although the AWHQ ultimately went bankrupt and closed its doors, it helped solidify Austin's reputation as a center of great music.

For people that find real-life longhorn cattle not quite big enough…the world's largest statue of a longhorn can be seen on the streets of Austin.

The fiberglass bovine is 12 feet high and 17 feet long, with a 9-foot horn spread.

In 1836, the Republic of Texas had its capital temporarily located in five different places: Washington-on-the-Brazos, Harrisburg, Galveston, Velasco, and Columbia.

In 1837, President Sam Houston moved the capital to the city named for him.

In 1839, President Mirabeau B. Lamar decided to relocate the government to a settlement called Waterloo, which he renamed Austin.

When President Houston was elected for his second term, he decided to move the capital back to Houston.

This prompted the brief and bloodless Archive War.

To maintain their town's status as capital of the Republic, the people of Austin chased down Houston's men, took the government papers at gunpoint, returned home, and hid them.

It was an effective gambit.

Houston (the man) never managed to move the government, and Houston (the city) never became the capital again.

The current Texas State Capitol building in Austin was completed in 1888.

Constructed of granite, it was advertised as the world's seventh-largest building at the time, with 393 rooms.

Its dome is about 15 feet higher than the nation's Capitol Dome, and it is the largest state capitol in the country.

The last President of the Republic of Texas, Anson Jones, is known as the Architect of Annexation.

His deft political and diplomatic maneuvering provided a real choice to Texas, which had been struggling as an independent country for a decade.

By playing all sides against each other, Jones not only encouraged the U.S. Congress to approve the annexation of Texas as a state, which meant certain war with Mexico, he also oversaw a peace agreement with Mexico that would have left Texas an independent nation closely allied with Britain and France.

Public sentiment, however, was so strongly pro-annexation that Jones' success at generating both options caused his complete political disgrace.

Anson Jones' final act as president was to lower the flag of the Republic of Texas for the last time on February 19, 1846.

He never returned to public life, although he believed he would.

Instead, he slipped deeper and deeper into depression over the next dozen years.

In early 1858, he checked into Houston's Old Capitol hotel, which had in fact once served as the Republic's capitol.

On January 9th, Jones had dinner with a friend and announced, "My public career began in this house, and I have been thinking it might close here."

Later, the 59-year-old statesman who provided Texas with a choice of destinies returned to his room and shot himself to death.

William Vanderbilt, Oscar Wilde, Ulysses S. Grant, Rutherford B. Hayes, and Lady Bird Johnson all have at least one thing in common: they were once guests at the Excelsior Hotel in Jefferson.

The hotel has been in constant operation since the 1850s, when Jefferson was a port city for riverboat traffic. The river traffic disappeared forever when a natural log dam on the Red River broke and drained all the water from Cypress Bayou.

The demise of the town fulfilled the prophecy made by railroad tycoon Jay Gould. After his offer to run track through town was rejected, Gould is said to have scrawled in the Excelsior's register, "The End of Jefferson."

Today, Gould's ornate private railcar, the *Atalanta*, sits across the street from the hotel, open to tourists.

If an African safari sounds like fun—except for the part about going to Africa—the Fossil Rim Wildlife Center near Glen Rose provides an alternative.

Working with a worldwide network of wildlife conservation organizations, the 1,700-acre center is home to more than a thousand animals roaming free, while humans drive through slowly to watch them.

There is also a lodge and a campsite on the grounds, providing two very different kinds of overnight experiences.

Residents of Fossil Rim include some of the world's most endangered animals, like white rhino, cheetah, and Grevy's zebra.

TEXAS
FACTS

As a contrasting experience to Fossil Rim, a riverbed in nearby Dinosaur Valley State Park offers a glimpse of footprints left by animals that did *not* escape extinction—some of the best-preserved dinosaur tracks in the world.

Dinosaur tracks are fairly prevalent throughout a strip of central Texas, although not in the other regions.

Western Texas is made of rock that was already solid when the giant reptiles roamed.

Land in the high plains and Gulf Coast regions was deposited after the dinosaurs were already gone.

Central Texas has land that was just the right age to record the dinosaurs' footsteps.

Waco was once the stomping grounds of the Columbian mammoth, an extinct version of a giant elephant.

Researchers have found the remains of more than 20 of the ancient animals, along with bones from a camel and a saber-tooth cat from the same era.

Scientists speculate that the remains are more than 50,000 years old, and that the animals died when they were trapped by flood waters and drowned.

exas has more fresh water than the "Land of 10,000 Lakes" (Minnesota), but it also has its own desert-scape, in the Monahans Sandhills State Park.

There are hundreds of miles of sand dunes in Texas, and most of them are fairly stable because of the vegetation. The dunes at Sandhills, however, are a bit more dynamic, growing and moving in response to the weather. Some of the dunes are as high as 70 feet, which provides some exciting terrain for sand-surfing.

To round off the whole desert experience, camel treks are available for the truly adventurous.

**T**he use of camels in the Texas desert is not a recent development.

In 1855, Jefferson Davis, then the U.S. Secretary of War, got Congress to allocate money to field-test the beasts of burden. The animals excelled in carrying, enduring without water, and traveling long distances through miserable conditions.

By the end of the Civil War, although the camels had proven efficient for both sides, they fell out of favor.

The animals smelled quite bad, frightened the horses, and had truly terrible personalities.

And so ended the dromedary era in the American southwest.

In 1876, salesman John Warne Gates rented Military Plaza in San Antonio, constructed a barbed-wire corral there, and loaded it with cattle. The spectacle of all those longhorns contained by this new wonder-product generated more orders for wire than could be produced by the company that had sent Gates to Texas.

He decided to strike off on his own and made a fortune in the steel business, capitalizing on the success of steel barbed wire. Later, he parlayed that into more, with investments in railroads and oil, ultimately launching the company that became Texaco.

The Devil's Rope Museum, about 75 miles east of Amarillo, is dedicated to the history of barbed wire, which some maintain was the tool that tamed the West.

Exhibits include various samples of wire, a collection of "Fence Maker Devices," and demonstrations of how to make barbed wire.

Texas is the salt of the earth. Literally.

Long before the Europeans arrived, the natives were getting their salt from the lakes and springs of the High Plains and using it to cure their meats.

The salt domes along the Gulf Coast and in eastern Texas are still huge, but most of the salt produced in the state comes from brine wells—natural sources of underground salt water.

Some estimate that salt accounts for 5 percent of the considerable mineral value of the state!

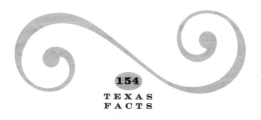

efore any discussion of chili begins, one thing must be made clear: Texas chili does *not* contain beans. There's meat. There's chili peppers. And everything else is an add-on. That's why it's called *chili con carne*, which is Spanish for "chili with meat."

Now that *that's* settled...

San Antonio is traditionally considered the birthplace of chili, and German immigrant Wilhelm Gebhardt is credited with creating chili *powder* in 1890. His invention made it possible for anyone, anywhere, at anytime to make a satisfying "bowl of red."

Gebhardt is also the Texan who, in 1911, wrote the first Mexican cookbook to be sold in the United States.

The Texas Legislature designated *chili* as the Official State Dish in 1977.

In 1997, the *chiltepin* was named the Official State "Native" Pepper, not to be confused with the *jalapeño*, which was named the Official State Pepper in 1995. Both are ingredients in Texas chili.

The chiltepin pepper is extremely hot, rating 50,000 to 100,000 Scoville units.

*Dr Pepper*, which is also native to Texas, is not hot at all.

*Dr Pepper*, the soft drink, was invented by a pharmacist in Waco in 1885. He had noticed that people loved the sweet smell of the soda fountain in the store and he was trying to capture that sensation in a taste.

By 1891, the drink was being produced at a bottling plant in Dublin, a few miles away, and it became a national hit in 1904 at the St. Louis World's Fair.

Today, the Dublin plant still makes *Dr Pepper* (there has been *no period* after "Dr" since the 1950s) according to the original formula—with cane sugar instead of corn syrup.

Waco's Dr Pepper Museum is a storehouse of information and memorabilia about the soft-drink industry in general *and* the headquarters of the Free Enterprise Institute, which teaches students about entrepreneurship.

If it weren't for Texas, there might not be any fancy French wines today.

In the late 19th century, a deadly infestation of phylloxera (a microscopic root-louse) threatened to wipe out all of Europe's vineyards.

Enter Thomas Volney Munson from Denison. Munson was a horticulturalist who developed more than 300 different grape varieties for growing in the United States.

He found one that was resistant to the nasty, vine-eating bug threatening the world's grape supply, grafted some of his super-stock to the European vines, and voilà!

The world was once again safe for bacchanalian delights, and Munson earned the Chevalier du Mérite Agricole from the French Legion of Honor.

Today, the T.V. Munson Viticulture Enology Center in Denison honors his memory and teaches the current crop of award-winning Texas winemakers.

he Texas Hill Country has its own rapidly growing wine region—growing both in size and reputation.

More than 280 family-owned vineyards cover 2,500 acres in the state, and with more than 180 wineries, Texas is the fifth-largest wine-producing state in the United States.

Finding a bottle outside the Lone Star state may not be all that easy, however.

In 2008, 95 percent of the two-and-a-half million gallons of wine produced in Texas was consumed in Texas.

The "Order of the Purple Foot" is an annual wine-stomping event in New Braunfels.

Couples work against the clock to produce as much juice as possible, with one person stomping on the grapes and the other one collecting the nectar.

The couple with the most juice wins, entitling them to have their names placed on a permanent plaque at the Dry Comal Creek Vineyards, where the event takes place.

All participants' names are printed on the label of that season's "Foot Pressed" wine.

S ome men are born to greatness.

Others rise to greatness through hard work and dedication.

John Milkovisch was just having a few beers with family and friends at his home in Houston.

Well, actually, it was more than 50,000 beers, and he never threw away any of the cans.

Instead, he flattened them and turned them into aluminum siding for his house, which is now owned by Houston's Orange Show Center for Visionary Art.

The project began in 1968, when John "got sick of mowing the grass" and began laying concrete—inlaid with marbles, rocks, and metal pieces—that covered his entire front and back yards.

A modest man, John never considered his work "art." He said it was just an enjoyable pastime, which he continued to work on until his death in 1988.

"Let my children plant at the head of my grave a pecan tree and at my feet an old-fashioned walnut tree. And when these trees shall bear, let the pecans and the walnuts be given out among the plain people so that they may plant them and make Texas a land of trees."

Such was the last request of former Texas Governor James Stephen Hogg in 1906, and so it came to pass. In fact, not only were the fruits of the trees on the governor's grave distributed throughout Texas, but the pecan tree was later named the Official State Tree of Texas.

In 1969, the trees were replaced with new ones, so Governor Hogg's wishes will continue to be carried out for years to come.

What can a Texan do with a thousand pounds of pecans?

If a proportional amount of flour, eggs, and sugar are also on hand, the El Paso Diablos baseball club proved they can bake a very big pie.

In 1999, their record-setting pie measured 50 feet across and weighed more than 20 tons.

No word is available on the current status of leftovers.

The Official State Flower of Texas is the Bluebonnet.

More than 5,000 different species of wildflowers bloom alongside Texas highways each spring, and it is no accident.

The state's Department of Transportation buys and sows about 30,000 pounds of wildflower seeds every year.

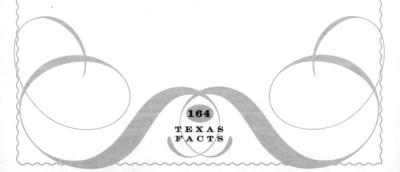

Ever at the forefront of finding homes for orphaned roads, Texas was the first state to establish an Adopt-a-Highway program.

The Civitan Club of Tyler was the first group to volunteer, adopting a two-mile stretch of Highway 69 in 1985.

In fact, the day that highway was adopted, March 9, has since become International Adopt-a-Highway Day.

The AMBER Alert System, used as an early notification system to help find abducted children, is a Texas innovation.

The first one was established in 1996 in Dallas/Fort Worth.

Although AMBER stands for "America's Missing: Broadcast Emergency Response," the system was named after nine-year-old Amber Hagerman, who was kidnapped and killed in Arlington, Texas.

People who go to Texas and "see the light" are not alone.

The "Marfa lights," seen between the town of Marfa and the Paisano Pass, have been mystifying people for more than a hundred years.

The first historical record of an unexplained glow in the region dates back to an 1883 cattle drive.

The lights still frequently dance across the sky, but no one has ever found their source.

Instead, the Texas State Highway Department has built a viewing area on U.S. Highway 90, so motorists can watch the show.

The Old Bragg Road to Saratoga, in the middle of the Big Thicket, was originally a rail bed for the old Santa Fe line.

Ghost hunters since the early 20th century have reported seeing a mysterious shining, which is referred to as the "Big Thicket Light" or the "Saratoga Light."

Although speculation abounds as to its cause, the origin of the light still eludes scientific explanation.

The world's largest bat colony spends its summer at Bracken Bat Cave near San Antonio, and every night, people come to watch as many as

20 million Mexican free-tailed bats come out in the evening.

The cave itself is not open to the general public, but members of Bat Conservation International, which cares for the property, are occasionally allowed to enter for a closer view of the colony emerging like bats out of...Bracken.

Right in the middle of Austin, under the Congress Avenue Bridge, 1.5 million Mexican free-tailed bats sleep all day, waiting for dusk and the chance to spend a night on the town.

Like paparazzi waiting for celebrities, tourists gather on top of the bridge and below it to watch the flying mammals leave home en masse looking for something to eat.

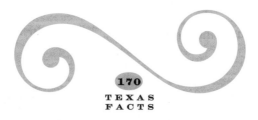

Jackie Bibby bills himself as the Texas Snake Man, and he has the world records to back up the claim. Here's one not to try at home: Bibby sat for 45 minutes in a bathtub with 87 rattlesnakes. Where? Texas, of course! Dublin, to be exact.

Bibby was born in Rising Star and has appeared on reality TV shows broadcast in countries all around the world.

Did we mention not to try this at home?

The Texas Cowboy-Poetry Gathering began in 1987 in Alpine to "promote, preserve, and practice" the story-telling arts of the American West.

On a Friday and Saturday in late February or early March, the rough and tumble icons of a bygone era gather to show their softer sides with poetry readings and cowboy music performances.

Activities like a celebrity roping and a raffle are part of the fun.

Then festivities end with a cowboy church service on Sunday morning.

Every year since 1855, singers converge on Henderson for the East Texas Sacred Harp Singing Convention. The term "sacred harp" refers to the human voice, and the songs sung are four-part hymns and anthems traditional of the American frontier.

**O**ther annual Texas events include...

- The World's Largest Rattlesnake Roundup, Sweetwater
- Texas Onion Fest, Weslaco
- Texas SandFest, Port Aransas (serves as a qualifying contest for the World Championship of Sand Sculpture)
- Old Settler's Music Festival, Austin
- Championship Fiddlers Frolic, Hallettsville
- National Polka Festival, Ennis
- Scottish Gathering of the Clans & Highland Games, Salado
- World Championship Muleshoe Pitching Contest, Muleshoe
- National Cow Calling Championships, Miami

exas-sized and free! That's the offer the Big Texan Steak Ranch in Amarillo has been making since the 1960s.

Anyone who can eat a 72-ounce steak in under an hour doesn't have to pay for it.

There's a special table for those interested in trying, with web-cams set up so the whole world can watch.

A lengthy tabulation of customers, from teens to seniors, who have managed to consume four-and-a-half pounds of beef and live to tell the tale can be found on the Internet.

A giant cowboy out front makes the restaurant easy to find.

By the way, failure to finish the steak within the time limit costs $72.

Bon appétit.

The Texas State Fair gave birth to the corn dog in 1942, when vendors deep-fried a hotdog covered in sweet corn batter and sold it for 15 cents.

Ever since, the only limit on what can be fried, sold, and eaten at the Fair is the imagination. And every year, that limit is stretched a little further.

Fried pralines? Check.

Fried peanut butter, banana, and jelly sandwich? Check.

But fried Coca-Cola? Yup! Ever since 2006.

Here's how it's done:

Flavor the batter with Coke, fry it, drizzle some Coke syrup, cover it with whipped cream and cinnamon sugar, and put a cherry on top!

In Texas, if you fry it, they will come...

## "Any Day Above Ground Is A Good One"

That's the slogan of the National Museum of Funeral History in Houston.

The museum claims to be the largest collector of funeral memorabilia and educational center on funeral heritage in the world.

Exhibits include historic hearses, fantasy coffins, and a full-scale replica of Pope John Paul II's crypt.

ene Roddenberry was born in El Paso and buried in space.

Roddenberry created *Star Trek*—the TV shows, the movies, the franchise, et al.

When he died in 1991, his body was cremated.

In 1997, a portion of his ashes were among those sent into orbit aboard a Pegasus rocket launched near the Canary Islands, the first "burial" in space. The capsule containing the ashes burned on re-entry into the Earth's atmosphere.

Celestis, the company that conducts space-burials, is based in Houston.

Early Spanish explorers in West Texas found a river so full of freshwater mollusk shells they named it, simply, Concho (shell) River. When they discovered that those mussels contained natural pearls, they went into business.

Only 5 percent of today's pearls are found in nature. (The others are "cultured.")

Concho pearls, found only in the rivers and lakes around the Texas city of San Angelo, are even more rare because of their beautiful colors—from pink to purple; from orange to green.

In the mid-17th century, the Spanish harvested the pearls and sent them back home, where some of them are said to have wound up in Spain's Crown Jewels.

In April 1554, three Spanish cargo/passenger ships ran aground on Padre Island. Nearly 300 passengers and crew died, and a fortune in gold and silver bound for Spain was lost.

The remains, discovered in 1967, are the oldest shipwrecks discovered off the U.S. coast.

The Corpus Christi Museum of Science and History now serves as curator of the artifacts (including some gold and silver coins), which are available for public viewing.

The 624 miles of Texas coastline contain more than 600 historic shipwrecks, including...

- the USS *Hatteras*, the iron-hulled steamer of the Civil War era that was sunk in battle in 1863 and discovered more than one hundred years later,

- the 1989 find of the remains of the iron-hull steamship *Mary*, which ran aground at Aransas Pass in 1876,

- the 1995 recovery of the French ship *Belle*, sailed by explorer Rene Robert Cavelier de La Salle in 1684, and

- the *Caroline*, a Civil War-era shipwreck revealed off the Texas coast by Hurricane Ike in 2009.

Scuba divers, meet Dr. Strangelove. At the former missile site dubbed Valhalla, the Cold War has been replaced by cold water (60° F), which now fills the missile silo. A dive shop in Midland offers an opportunity to explore the historic cylinder with a mask, tank, and fins.

Divers enter through the blast doors, suit-up below the escape shaft, and dive into water about 135 feet deep— presumably a safer use of the site than what was originally intended.

The fact that a 10-gallon hat actually holds less than a gallon of water is *not* disproof of a Texas braggart. The whole thing was just a misunderstanding.

It's not gallon. It's *galón*.

The word is Spanish for braid, the standard decoration above the brim of the iconic headgear worn by *true* Texans everywhere.

**B**efore 1978, Dallas was a city in Texas. Then, CBS aired a primetime soap opera with the same name, about a rich oil family, and the word took on a whole new meaning.

The series ran for 13 years, with a few reunion movies produced after that. The name "Dallas" became synonymous with conspicuous consumption and cut-throat social intrigue set at a place called Southfork Ranch.

outhfork Ranch, where *Dallas* was filmed, was a real ranch, where real people lived. But throngs of fans came from around the world to see the home of the *fictional* TV characters, and the real residents had to move.

In 1985, Southfork became a full-time tourist attraction. It still caters today to former viewers who come to "relive" their favorite moments at the place where none of it ever really happened.

Larry Hagman, who starred as "J.R. Ewing" in *Dallas*, was a native Texan, born in Fort Worth. He was the only actor to appear in 356 of the 357 shows that aired.

Hagman's mother, Mary Martin, was also born in Texas—Weatherford, Texas. She was a stage and movie star, best remembered as having played the title role in *Peter Pan* on Broadway. She won a Tony award for that performance, and another for her performance in *Sound of Music*.

It should come as no surprise that the term *maverick* comes from Texas, but it wasn't originally meant as a compliment.

In 1847, Sam Maverick was a lawyer who accepted a herd of cattle as payment for his services, but he wasn't much interested in becoming a rancher. In fact, he left a slave in charge of the herd and moved to the city.

By himself, the slave didn't have much chance of conducting a roundup or branding any of the cattle, so they pretty much roamed free.

Thus, a *maverick* came to refer to any head of beef that didn't have a brand on the hide.

Today, the term has lost the connotation of benign neglect and conveys more a sense of the trailblazer.

On the day after Christmas, in 1908, Jack Johnson defeated Tommy Burns to become the heavyweight boxing champion of the world.

The Galveston native, who had survived the Great Storm of 1900, was the first black athlete to break the color barrier.

Although his hometown had originally scheduled a victory parade and celebration for Johnson, the event was cancelled when local leaders learned that Johnson had married a white woman.

Today, Jack Johnson Boulevard in Galveston memorializes the champ.

While he was still the world champion, Jack Johnson was arrested for violation of the Mann Act, a federal law making it illegal to transport women across state lines for "immoral purposes."

The woman in question was Johnson's girlfriend, whom he married later the same year, but the prosecution was prompted more by the colors of their skin (his black; hers white) than the morality of their activities.

Nevertheless, Jackson spent a year at Leavenworth.

While he was there, the champ invented a tool to loosen fastening devices.

When he was released from prison, he applied for and received a U.S. patent for his special wrench.

The presence of baseball in Texas dates back to at least 1861, with the formation of the Houston Base Ball Club.

The first recorded game was in 1868, at the San Jacinto Battlegrounds near Houston, where the Houston Stonewalls defeated the Galveston Robert E. Lees, 35 to 2.

Perhaps as a way of posing the question, "What's in a name?" the Houston baseball team that helped found the Texas League in 1888 was called the Babies.

Perhaps as a way of answering the question, the team name changed by 1907 to the Buffalos, which was shortened to the Buffs.

In baseball, a "Texas Leaguer," also known as a "bloop single," is a ball that is weakly hit but falls between the infielders and the outfielders for a base hit.

When major league baseball came to Houston in 1962, the new team was called the Colt .45's.

They became the Astros three years later, when the team moved to the first domed stadium for a major league team, nicknamed the Astrodome.

In 1972, the Washington Senators moved to the Dallas/Ft. Worth area, to become the Texas Rangers.

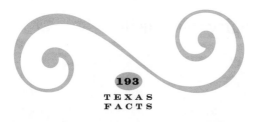

**H**all of Fame pitcher Nolan Ryan was born in Refugio. He was drafted by the New York Mets in 1965 and retired from the field in 1993 as a Texas Ranger. Throughout his career, he was known for his blazing fastball and his habit of breaking records.

He pitched more no-hitters (seven) and strikeouts (5,714) than anyone else, by a wide margin.

He became the president of the Rangers in 2008, in addition to being the Chairman of the Board of a bank and a cattle rancher.

In 2010, Ryan led an investment group that purchased the team in a federal bankruptcy court auction.

Of the first forty-four Super Bowls, the Dallas Cowboys appeared in eight and won five.

Dallas' Cowboys Stadium was chosen to host the forty-fifth Super Bowl.

The Houston Oilers, which was one of the original American Football League teams in 1962, left Texas for Tennessee in 1997.

The replacement team, the Houston Texans, became the first NFL expansion team to win its debut in 2002 by beating the Dallas Cowboys 19-10.

The rodeo is the official state sport of Texas and the first one ever held was in Pecos in 1883.

The West of the Pecos Rodeo is an annual affair now, and it lays claim to being the descendant of that first rodeo.

Legend has it that the whole thing evolved out of a contest between two ranch hands—Trav Windham and Morg Livingston.

Both had good professional reputations and people wanted to know who was best.

Each is said to have won at least one event, before talented cowboys who had originally come from all over the territory just to watch found themselves involved in contests riding broncos and roping cattle.

exarkana is a town in two states.

The border of Texas and Arkansas cuts right through the middle of town.

Legally, that means there are really *two* towns—Texarkana, TX, and Texarkana, AR—with two city governments.

But they share a post office...and a fire department... In fact, Texarkana *operates* as a single town.

As for the name: **Tex**—*TEX*as; **Ark**—*ARK*ansas; **Ana**—Louisi*ANA*.

Never mind that Louisiana is 30 miles away. Why should that part of the story be any less confusing?

## ABOUT THE AUTHOR

Victor Dorff is a New Yorker living in Southern California and writing about the travel destinations that make the world such an interesting place to visit. His work has been seen on television, on the web, and on bookshelves around the country. He can be seen in airports, hotels, museums, restaurants, or any-where there is a good story being told.